...!

...ter

...y computer technicians does it take
to screw in a lightbulb?

Why did the computer go to the shoe store?

What do you call a girl who prefers her
computer to her boyfriend?

What do computers do for fun?

**TO ACCESS THE RIOTOUS ANSWERS,
OPEN THIS BOOK AND PLUG INTO
A POTPOURRI OF POTENT
PC PUNMANIA!**

*THE OFFICIAL
COMPUTER FREAKS
JOKE BOOK*

BOOKS BY LARRY WILDE

The Official Wasp Joke Book
The Official All America Joke Book
The *Ultimate* Lawyers Joke Book
The *Ultimate* Jewish Joke Book
More The Official Doctors Joke Book
The Official Executives Joke Book
The Official Sports Maniacs Joke Book
The *Absolutely Last* Official Sex Maniacs Joke Book
The Official Book of John Jokes
The Official Politicians Joke Book
The Official Rednecks Joke Book
The *Last* Official Smart Kids Joke Book
The *Absolutely Last* Official Polish Joke Book
The *Last* Official Irish Joke Book
The *Last* Official Sex Maniacs Joke Book
The Larry Wilde Book of Limericks
The Official Lawyers Joke Book
The Official Doctors Joke Book
More The Official Sex Maniacs Joke Book
The *Last* Official Jewish Joke Book

also

The Official Bedroom/Bathroom Joke Book
More The Official Smart Kids/Dumb Parents Joke Book
The Official Book of Sick Jokes
More The Official Jewish/Irish Joke Book
The *Last* Official Italian Joke Book
The Official Cat Lovers/Dog Lovers Joke Book
The Official Dirty Joke Book
The *Last* Official Polish Joke Book
The Official Golfers Joke Book
The Official Smart Kids/Dumb Parents Joke Book
The Official Religious/Not So Religious Joke Book
More The Official Polish/Italian Joke Book
The Official Black Folks/White Folks Joke Book
The Official Virgins/Sex Maniacs Joke Book
The Official Jewish/Irish Joke Book
The Official Polish/Italian Joke Book

and in hardcover

THE LARRY WILDE LIBRARY OF LAUGHTER
THE COMPLETE BOOK OF ETHNIC HUMOR
HOW THE GREAT COMEDY WRITERS CREATE LAUGHTER
THE GREAT COMEDIANS TALK ABOUT COMEDY

THE OFFICIAL COMPUTER FREAKS JOKE BOOK

Larry Wilde and Steve Wozniak

BANTAM BOOKS

TORONTO • NEW YORK • LONDON • SYDNEY • AUCKLAND

THE OFFICIAL COMPUTER FREAKS JOKE BOOK

A Bantam Book / January 1989

ISBN 0-553-27726-X

Published simultaneously in the United States and Canada

Bantam Books are published by Bantam Books, a division of Bantam Doubleday Dell Publishing Group, Inc. Its trademark, consisting of the words "Bantam Books" and the portrayal of a rooster, is Registered in U.S. Patent and Trademark Office and in other countries. Marca Registrada. Bantam Books, 666 Fifth Avenue, New York, New York 10103.

PRINTED IN THE UNITED STATES OF AMERICA

O   0 9 8 7 6 5 4 3 2 1

*To the wonderful
mother of Woz
and
Maryruth*

With Special Thanks To

William Ackerman . . . John Barry . . . Jack E. Brown . . . Jane Jordan Browne . . . Karen Bjorkman . . . John Buttles, P.E. . . . Dick Davies . . . Sandra Engle . . . Chris Efendaki . . . Doris R. Hart . . . Kathy Hall . . . Jay Krone . . . Marilyn Kushner . . . Cora Matheson . . . Frank J. McHugh . . . Judy Malloy . . . Carole Terwilliger Meyers . . . Alleen, Don, and Kelvin Nilsen . . . Diana Gil-Passolas . . . Robert A. Pease . . . Trace Pratten . . . Brian Rouff . . . Kerry Rapp . . . John Raleigh . . . Alfonso Qwerty . . . Richard Ramella . . . David M. Sanders . . . Jack Stanley . . . Gerard W. Schoenwald . . . William Travis . . . Leonard W. Williams, C.P.A.

and

Mary Poulos Wilde

About the Authors

LARRY WILDE

This is the 41st "Official" joke book by Larry Wilde. With sales of more than ten million copies, it is the biggest selling humor series in publishing history.

Larry Wilde has been making people laugh for over thirty years. As a stand-up comedian, he has performed in top night spots with stars such as Debbie Reynolds, Pat Boone, and Ann-Margret.

His numerous television appearances include *The Tonight Show, The Today Show, Merv Griffin,* and *The Mary Tyler Moore Show.*

Larry's two books on comedy technique, *The Great Comedians Talk About Comedy* (Citadel) and *How the Great Comedy Writers Create Laughter* (Nelson-Hall), are acknowledged as the definitive works on the subject and are used as college textbooks.

A recognized authority on comedy, Larry is also a motivational speaker. In his humorous keynote speeches for corporations, associations, and healthcare facilities, he advocates getting more out of life by developing a better sense of humor.

Larry Wilde is the founder of National Humor Month, celebrated across the U.S. to point out the valuable contribution laughter makes to the quality of our lives. It begins each year on April Fools' Day.

He lives on the northern California coast with his wife, Maryruth.

STEVE WOZNIAK

Steve Wozniak has many interests, not the least of which are computers and jokes.

In 1973 he collaborated with Steve Jobs on a circuit board for a small advanced computer. At the same time he started San Jose's first dial-a-joke, operating it from his home answering machine.

The circuit board he designed with Jobs became Apple I, and Woz's interest in jokes was eclipsed by the astronomical success of his electronic inventions.

In 1977 he created Apple II, and the face of personal computer technology was changed forever.

In 1977, Woz founded UNUSON Corp. and produced two US Festival Rock/Country music extravaganzas, including technology exhibits—the first ever video simulcast with the Soviet Union.

Today, on behalf of Apple, he speaks to educational, hobby, and professional groups on topics related to small computers. He founded CL9, a Los Gatos, California, company specializing in the development of remote control home appliances, and he's active in numerous civic projects.

Woz lives in the secluded Santa Cruz Mountains where he now can indulge his love of jokes.

This is his first collaboration on a joke book.

Contents

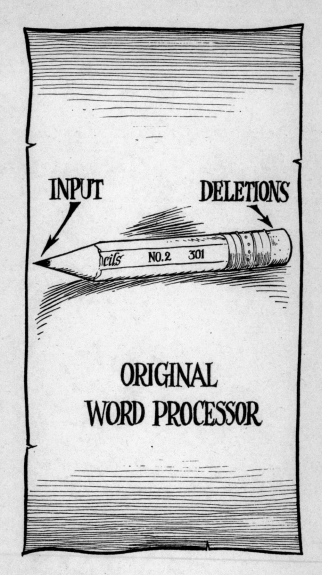

INPUT

DELETIONS

ORIGINAL
WORD PROCESSOR

Introduction

Never before in the history of mankind has a technology enveloped the world as quickly as the little machine that stores and provides information. And as the growth of the computer industry spirals upward, its humorous side is beginning to come to the fore.

Of course, computer humor hasn't had time to catch up to other topics that have been ripe for ridicule for centuries, such as golf, which was introduced over five hundred years ago, or sex, which was introduced in the Garden of Eden. Then again, maybe the computer *was* introduced in Paradise!

Why is Eve considered the first computer operator?
She had an Apple in one hand and a Wang in the other.

When the Women's Rights movement began, the feminists couldn't see anything funny about themselves or the way they were going about trying to accomplish their goals. Today they're less uptight about it, and many of them can now laugh at their peccadilloes.
The same thing is beginning to happen in the computer industry:

Did you hear about the programmer whose doctor told him he needed more exercise, so he started to roll his own joints?

Once the hackers and programmers and the design engineers see the funny side of their business, the floodgates will open and the guffaws will thunder across the land.
Right now the computer industry has a wide scope with jokes that appeal to the kids as well as the most sophisticated corporate exec. Here's a riddle the kids love to tell:

What kind of cookies do computers like?
Chocolate chip.

The programmers, recognized as the creative contributors to the industry, represent the highest level of abstract thinking. This kind of gag appeals to that unconventional group:

When I face that great computer in the sky, let it be written that though I was spindled and mutilated—I did not fold.

Some of the best computer fun has come from the corporate world. Inexperienced executives were catapulted into decision-making positions and were often left by the wayside. Many companies folded and upper management suffered the ignominy of failure. But the human spirit bounces back with humor. Take this example of exaggerated executive expertise:

A software salesman was cooling his heels in the outer office of the president of a major computer company. Just as he was about to be granted an audience, an old gypsy woman was ushered in ahead of him.

"What's she doing here?" complained the salesman.

"Oh," replied the secretary, "Mr. Craig only brings her in for the really important decisions."

But without question, the computer is here to stay. Just its ability to match up males and females and arrange their meeting demonstrates its usefulness to society. Here is a typical result:

Marty and Donna met through a computer dating service. This was their first date. As they drove through the quiet countryside, the motor began to pound and finally stopped. The worried boy turned to the girl and said, "Gee, I wonder what the knock could be?"

"Maybe," said the girl, "it's opportunity."

And now here's your opportunity to enjoy the very first collection of computer quips, jokes, and stories about corporate execs, engineers, salespeople, marketing VPs, hackers, and programmers.

Then, of course, there's the consumer. The buyer who made it possible for us to lampoon all those people. There's plenty of glee at the expense of the computer user too.

But start moving. Turn off your PC. Put

your printer to rest. Open the book and get
ready to interface with some high-speed,
high-tech hilarity.

Larry Wilde
Steve Wozniak

High-Tech High Jinks

What's the difference between a computer salesman and a used-car salesman?

The used-car salesman knows when he's lying.

• • •

The office manager called IBM and said, "You've got to come in and fix our computer."

"What seems to be the problem?" asked the service technician.

"Someone dropped a rubber band into it and it's been making snap decisions all morning."

• • •

1

COMPUTER

An electronic device that will never replace office workers until it learns how to spread gossip and laugh at the boss's jokes.

• • •

How many computer technicians does it take to screw in a light bulb?

Two. One to do it and one to tell him he's doing it wrong.

• • •

Have you heard about the new computer from Mexico?

You get salsa with your silicon chips.

• • •

What did Indians use to make their computers?

Buffalo chips.

• • •

COMPUTER

An invention that will never be the equal of man until it can put the blame for its mistakes on some other computer.

"Hip hip hooray for the ultra-violet and photo-gray"

3

What does an engineer say to his coworkers when he's leaving work for the day?

"I'm going home—oscillator."

• • •

King Abdul Omar Al Hassani, the wealthiest oil potentate in the world, decided to take his eight-year-old son to Disney World in Florida. He loved the boy dearly and would do anything for his happiness.

The king and the young prince left the Middle East, and when they arrived in Tampa, the boy said, "Father, this was a wonderful flight. I really like this airplane."

So the king bought the huge jet right on the spot for the little boy. He had United paint over their logo and prepare it for the flight home.

As they drove toward Disney World, the youngster spotted some men playing golf. "Oh, Father," said the boy, "that is something I'd really like to do." King Hassani picked up the limousine phone and immediately purchased the entire golf club for his darling son.

They finally arrived at Disney World and the eight-year-old was ecstatic. As they walked around, the boy said, "Oh, Father, please! I want a Mickey Mouse outfit!"

So the king bought him IBM.

• • •

Teacher to pupil: "This homework is a disgrace. I'd like a note from your computer."

• • •

What's a computer's favorite munchie? Chips and dip.

• • •

Kendall and his little boy stopped in front of a computer store and began peering in the window. "Daddy," said the child, "what's that TV screen for?"

"I don't really know, son."

"That looks like the keys on a typewriter," said the boy. "What's that used for?"

"I don't know."

"How does a computer work?"

"I don't know, son."

"Gosh, Dad, I'm sorry to bother you with all these questions."

"That's okay, son. How else do you expect to learn?"

• • •

SILICON SERENADE

"Somewhere Over the RAMbow"

5

**What do they use in computers in Idaho?
Potato Chips.**

• • •

What did the father computer say about his son?

"He's just a chip off the old block."

• • •

COMPUTER

A machine that can solve all kinds of numerical problems, except how to adjust the date of a woman's birth to her present age.

• • •

Want to have some fun? Send your record club a subscription from the book club and send the book club a subscription from your record club. Then see if the two computers will work out the billing.

• • •

"Which is faster, a computer or a human being?"

"Wait—let me think about that one."

• • •

What do you get if you cross a computer with a TV newscaster?

You get a hairy reasoner.

• • •

Did you know that the Cray Two is so fast it can do an infinite loop in two and a half seconds?

• • •

SIGN ON MAINFRAME

Beware of computer—it bytes.

• • •

Which way did the Texas programmer go?
He went data way.

• • •

Why did the robot eat quarters at noon?
It was his lunch money.

• • •

Have you heard the new computer song?
It's called "My Heart Belongs to Data."

• • •

Did you hear about the new Chinese computer?
An hour later, you have to program it again.

Ron Dentinger, the wonderful Wisconsin wit, loves this wacky wheezer:

In the early fifties, when the first computer came out, only the U.S. government could afford it. The machine was so large it required an entire building just to house it.

Once the computer was in place, the Pentagon prepared to give it a test run. The top generals proposed a mock battle. They gave the computer all the information that could be pertinent in the battle: troop strength, ammunition, available equipment, time of day, etc.

After the information was entered, the generals asked the computer, "Should we attack from the north or should we attack from the east?"

The computer's lights flashed on and off. There was a steady hum and strong vibrations as it worked over the problem. After what seemed like hours, the thing printed out its solution: "Yes."

"Yes, what?" demanded one of the generals.

The computer replied, "Yes, sir!"

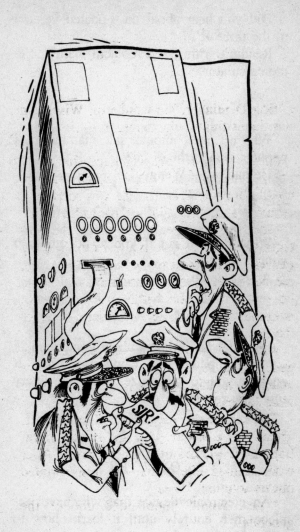

• • •

Did you hear about the updated version of the three R's?

Readin', 'ritin', and replacin' batteries in the calculator.

• • •

Why was the computer salesman the most popular man at the disco?

He had a big Wang.

• • •

What do you get if you're not good to your Apple?

A crab apple.

• • •

"What's the big deal about computers?"

"A computer is a wonderful thing. It enables you to recognize a mistake every time you repeat it."

• • •

COMPUTER

An electronic device that will never replace men entirely until it learns how to strike for shorter hours.

• • •

BUMPER STICKER

Old Programmers Never Die—
They Just Lose Their Memories.

• • •

Abigail was having a hard time operating her desktop computer. It was apparent she had reached the end of her patience when she muttered at the screen, "I know one thing. If I had a glass face like yours, I'd sure behave better."

• • •

"I got this terrific deal on our new computer," Harold explained to his wife. "The salesman said I'd get used to the red screen and purple characters in no time at all."

• • •

Did you hear about the new computer that's so human that on Monday mornings it comes in late?

• • •

There's another in California that's so human that when it goes down, they give it wine coolers and vitamin C.

• • •

Ed McManus, the Massachusetts genius behind *The Jokesmith,* America's funniest gag supplier, whipped up this whimsical winner:

Delbert and Fletch, two industrial robots, escaped from the engineering lab. It was Saturday night and they decided to pick up some girls.

The boys agreed to separate, then meet later on the corner of Main and Broadway with their dates.

Two hours passed and Delbert arrived at the appointed spot. He found Fletch standing in front of a mailbox and a fire alarm.

"Who are your two friends?" asked Delbert.

"Forget them," sighed Fletch. "The short fat one with the big mouth just stands there, and if you touch the redhead, she screams her lungs out!"

• • •

COMPUTER

A machine that works faster than people, because it never stops to answer the telephone.

• • •

"But Miss Krumm, you can't retire. You're
the only one who knows how to spell!"

15

Did you hear about the computer that drinks?

They're calling it Uniswacked!

 •   •   •

COMPUTER PROGRAMMING PRINCIPLES

1. The computer is never wrong.
2. If the computer is wrong, see Rule #1.

 •   •   •

What does an electron say when it meets resistance?

"I'm going ohm."

 •   •   •

Why do computers like human beings?

Why do you think? Human beings turn them on.

 •   •   •

Larsen stormed into the office with a worried look on his face. "The computer's broken down!" he exclaimed. "Does anybody remember how to think?"

 •   •   •

Expose yourself to a computer.

Jim Warren, the talented high-tech Pied Piper, tells this titillater:

A bank robber decided to knock over a fully computerized bank. He pushed a note into the automatic teller machine that read, "Put the money in the bag, sucker, or I'll blow your circuits out."

The machine shoved back this message: "Straighten your tie, sucker. I'm taking your picture."

"It's quite simple, really," said the chiropractor to his patient. "You've been sitting in front of the computer so long, you've developed a floppy disk."

• • •

COMPUTER NERD

A guy who knows 147 technically possible ways to have sex but doesn't know any women.

• • •

A flying saucer landed in New Jersey, and the state police promptly arrested the three Martians on board. They were taken to a nearby IBM headquarters in an attempt to have the computers work out a means of communication.

Stocker, an engineer, said, "My engineering logic suggests that I learn their language and question them for you."

"Hold on," said Pesta, a programmer. "My programming insights suggest that I teach them English and we question them in our own language."

Just then the sales VP grabbed one of the little Martians and started to drag him out of the room. "Wait a minute!" shouted Stocker. "Where are you going?"

"In the next room," sneered the sales

exec. "I'm going to beat this little bugger until he talks!"

• • •

What do you call the fastest computer in the world?

A presto digitator.

• • •

Eva Wofsy, the fabulous Florida insurance exec, provided this perfect pearl:

Before Gordon Cooper ascended in his memorable flight into space, he was approached by a reporter and asked, "How do you feel?"

"I feel terrible," replied the astronaut. "I'm worried."

"But look what you're doing for your country, your family, posterity. What've you got to be worried about?"

Said Cooper, "There are one thousand gadgets in this computer, and each one has been made by the lowest bidder."

• • •

Should you be afraid of a computerized dog?

No. Its bark is worse than its byte.

• • •

What do you get if you cross a computer and a Doberman?

A computer that pees on fire hydrants.

• • •

What happens if you punch your computer too hard?

It goes down for the count.

• • •

Why did the computer go to the shoe store?

To get rebooted.

• • •

COMPUTER

A mathematical brain that can figure out all kinds of problems except the things in this world that just don't add up.

• • •

What do programmers have in common with spies?

They both write in code.

• • •

What's black and white and red all over?

A printout from Russia.

• • •

The new computer was attempting to translate from English into Russian. It was doing fine until the operator typed in "Out of sight, out of mind."

The Russian translation: "Invisible insanity."

• • •

"At least in Hell it's too hot for these suckers!"

The Soviet Union has just developed a microcomputer that they brag is the biggest microcomputer in the world.

• • •

Why did the computer go to the grocery store?
To buy cheese for its mouse.

• • •

What do you get when you cross an ocelot with an alligator?
An oscillator.

• • •

A German shepherd was out looking for a job. He passed an office with a sign that said:

WANTED
Experienced Worker who is
excellent typist, can operate
computer, and is bilingual.

"That's for me," thought the dog. He picked up the sign and walked into the office.
The astonished manager said, "Don't tell me you're applying for the job?"
"Woof," said the German shepherd, and he walked over to the typewriter and typed seventy-five words a minute without an er-

ror. Then he went to the computer and produced a perfect readout on the history of
dog breeding.

"Well, that's great," said the manager,
"but are you bilingual?"

"Meow! Meow!" said the dog.

Data Base Dating

Warner went to a computer dating bureau and picked out a lovely young woman from her photo. But they explained he couldn't meet her. He'd have to take out a gray-haired woman of sixty-three.

"Why a woman of sixty-three?" he asked.

"This is a union shop and she has seniority."

• • •

The dating computer was very active that day. A tall, handsome six-footer stood in front of it. "I'm a millionaire," he bragged. "I have twenty oil wells, a gold mine, and I run five banks." So the computer mugged him.

• • •

They tried an experiment at the university. All dates to the dance were arranged by a computer. After a rough evening, one student remarked, "What a frightening experience to find out just what you deserve."

• • •

Archie came back from the computer dating office. He told his roommate, "I asked for someone on the small side who's into water sports, formal dress, and doesn't talk too much."

"So what happened?"

"They fixed me up with a penguin."

• • •

They had met through a computer dating service. This was their third date.

"Darling," she whispered, "will you still love me after we are married?"

"I think so," he replied. "I've always been especially fond of married women."

"We'd like to get married, but her
system is not IBM compatible."

• • •

In a local Health, Education and Welfare office, a stack of punch cards was placed into a computerized sorting machine. The computer was then set to divide the cards according to sex. The result was five stacks of cards.

• • •

Dave Flannigam, the Test Systems Strategies Veep, loves this lulu:

Gloria was lamenting her relationships with men who were in the computer business. "They all seem intelligent and stimulating," she said, "but none of them can make love."

First there was the salesman who always promised but could never deliver. "But," he said, "you'll love it when you get it."

Next was a service technician who always said, "I know it looks bleak now, but don't worry, it'll be up tomorrow."

Finally, she dated a software engineer who created a detailed flowchart of the love-making process and then announced, "Frankly, I think you should just implement this yourself."

• • •

Charlie and Gus were having a cocktail after work. "I think," said Charlie, "dating through a computer can save a guy a lot of guesswork."

"Yeah," said Gus, "but so does a bikini."

• • •

LOSER

A guy whose computer dating service sends him the number of dial-a-prayer.

• • •

Rigby got out of the station wagon and went into a Silicon Valley motel office. "I have my wife and kids with me," he said to the clerk, "and before checking in, I want to be sure this is a family motel—not one of those places where couples come and go all night."

"Sir," replied the clerk, "this here is a respectable establishment. We wouldn't have nothin' to do with such goings-on."

"Fine," said the traveler, "what are your rates?"

"For the deluxe unit," said the clerk, "it's twenty dollars an hour."

• • •

Payton, a tall and very thin programmer, was so involved with his work that he never even thought about eating. Looking emaciated also made him very shy around women.

One day an attractive secretary from the sales department invited Payton to her apartment after work.

He arrived full of expectation, particularly after she removed his jacket, shirt, and tie and then led him into her bedroom.

There on a satin pillow lay a well-groomed French poodle. She led skinny Payton to the bed and then said to the dog, "See, Bitsy, this is what you're going to look like if you don't eat your Gravy Train!"

Dr. Fallon, the new intern, made his morning round of the San Jose maternity ward. All the women were unmarried, and all expected their babies the first week in February.

As he entered the ward, one woman left for the ladies' room. "I suppose Miss Marlow expects her baby in February, too?" the intern asked one of the unwed mothers-to-be.

"It's *Mrs.* Marlow, not Miss," he was told, "and we don't know when she's expecting her baby. She didn't go to the new contract celebration office party."

• • •

Tully and Stan were having a brew at a Pittsburgh pub.

"You're just not up to date on the electronic world," complained Tully.

"Believe me, I'm not prejudiced against automation," said Stan, "but I'd like to ask you one question about computers: Would you want your daughter to marry one?"

• • •

How do computers meet each other?
Through computer dating services.

• • •

"You will interface with a tall, dark, fully
compatible binary stranger."

Did you hear about the two computers that couldn't get together because of religious differences?

She's AC and he's DC.

• • •

What do you call a girl who'd rather be with her computer than her boyfriend?

An infomaniac.

• • •

Brian Brookes, the Cincinnati bon vivant, loves this nifty bauble:

A Massachusetts lawyer went to London to try to locate a young woman. Her father, who had been the CEO of an electronics firm, had died and left her a large fortune. The police were called in to assist in the search but were no help. The lawyer turned it over to a young, personable detective who specialized in computer crimes. Several weeks passed without any news, and the lawyer was beginning to feel concerned over the matter. Suddenly the young detective appeared and smilingly informed him he had located the heiress.

"Where is she?" asked the lawyer.

"At my place," replied the detective. "We were married yesterday."

• • •

Dexter sat down in the psychiatrist's office. "Now then," said the shrink, "what is it that brings you here?"

"Doctor, you've got to help me. I'm a computer programmer, and I've fallen in love with my computer. I realize, though, that I can't marry her."

"Well, I'm glad that you haven't lost your sense of reality."

"Oh, it could never work," said Dexter. "She wants a career."

• • •

It takes a brave hacker to admit his mistakes, especially during a paternity-suit hearing.

• • •

Harry, the production manager at a Silicon Valley chip factory, approached Dorothy, the shapeliest girl on the assembly line. "Hey, Dottie, here's a riddle," he said to her. "Why are you so popular?"

"Is it my complexion?" she asked.

"No," said Harry.

"My figure?"

"No."

"My personality?"

"No."

"I give up," said Dottie.

"That's it!"

"When I signed up for computer dating,
this is not what I had in mind."

• • •

There are many computer dating services these days. What's their purpose?

Friendchip and courtchip.

• • •

How would you describe a promiscuous girl you meet through a dating service?

One you can have a good time with even if you play your cards wrong.

• • •

Bo and Kent were sipping a glass of Gallo Chablis at the Peppermill.

"What's the matter?" asked Bo of his engineer buddy. "You look kind of down."

"My girlfriend told me that my lovemaking is just like a news bulletin."

"How's that?"

"Brief, unexpected, and usually a disaster."

• • •

Tim Coats cracks up friends with this corker:

The office was closed. Employees had all left for the day. The building was deserted. On the tenth floor a male computer whispered to a female computer, "Wow! Nice set of bits!"

• • •

Marilyn accepted Harvey's proposal of marriage, and the young hacker felt overjoyed and humble at his good fortune.

"I can't imagine why you'd have me," said Harvey. "I'm not much of a conversationalist about anything except computers, and I'm certainly not much to look at either."

"I thought of that," admitted Marilyn, "but I figure you'll be at the office most of the time."

• • •

What is the difference between an engineer and a mathematician?

One of each was posted at the end of a one-hundred-foot hallway. At the other end was a great-looking *Sports Illustrated* swimsuit model.

Rules: First one to reach the girl could have a date with her. The only restriction was that they were to advance in increments equal to half the remaining distance.

The mathematician turned and walked away because he knew he couldn't reach her.

The engineer started forward immediately because he knew he could get close enough for all practical purposes.

• • •

How do computers spend Saturday nights?
They go out on datas, of course.

"Just one teensy byte . . ."

• • •

Jarvis, a programmer, was having coffee with Melissa, a pretty sales rep, in the company cafeteria.

"Why don't we get married?" asked the electronics whiz.

"Are you kidding?" asked the girl. "You eat nothing but junk food, your clothes are a mess, you haven't shaved or showered in a week, and all you ever think about is computers."

"Well, nobody's perfect."

• • •

Priscilla was a twenty-eight-year-old unmarried software designer. She never seemed to have time to date or even meet eligible men.

Her mother suggested she place the following classified ad in the personals column of the San Jose *Mercury:*

Beautiful, successful computer exec would like to meet adventurous playboy who wants some fast action.

A week later, the mother asked, "Anybody answer the ad?"

"Just one," replied Priscilla.

"From who?"

"I can't tell you!"

"You've got to tell me!" screamed the mother.

"All right, if you must know. It was from Daddy."

• • •

Debbie's father was president of one of the most successful computer firms in Houston. His stock was worth over two hundred million dollars.

One night Debbie's date took her to a romantic restaurant and over after-dinner drinks said, "You're very rich, aren't you?"

"Yes," said the heiress.

"I'm very poor," he said, "but will you marry me anyway?"

"No."

"I didn't think you would."

"Then why did you ask?" asked Debbie.

"I just wanted to see what it was like to lose two hundred million dollars in one night."

• • •

Doreen, a computer programmer with a new boyfriend, was looking for ways to tell other suitors she was no longer available. "It's easy," said a coworker. "Just say your mode is single but your field option is taken."

• • •

43

JUST A QUESTION OF TIME

An electronic brain sitting in a cocktail lounge, telling a well-stacked computer: "Nobody understands me."

• • •

They each received a computer printout from the dating service, and this was their first date.

Bernie had shown Karen his stamp collection and just about everything else of interest in his apartment. He put Ravel's *Boléro* on the stereo, poured the last of the wine into their glasses, and said, "Karen, do you object to making love?"

"That's something I've never done," she replied.

"Never made love?"

"No, silly. Never objected."

Silicon Sillies

Why was William Tell's son electrocuted?
He forgot to unplug the Apple before his
father shot it off his head!

• • •

How many computer technicians does it
take to screw in a light bulb?
Only one if he can get a program written
for it.

SILICON VALLEY

Technology heaven with tract housing.

• • •

In spite of being weird, Flip was recognized by other hackers as being the best in the Valley. He dressed unusually, acted strangely, but still everyone respected him for his work.

One afternoon a motorcycle cop stopped Flip for speeding. As he wrote out the ticket, the officer noticed the backseat filled with seals. "You not only were doing eighty," said the surprised policeman, "but with all those animals back there you can barely see out the window. You better take those seals to the aquarium."

Next day Flip was stopped again for speeding by the same cop. The officer noticed the seals were still in the backseat, only now they were all wearing sunglasses.

"Hey," said the cop, "didn't I tell you to take those seals to the aquarium?"

"I did," said Flip, "and today I'm taking them to the beach!"

• • •

"CIAO!"

House Systems Chairman Steve Kirsch asks:

What's the toughest business in Silicon Valley?
Trying to rent vacant offices.

. . .

What do you get when you cross a computer with a parrot?
A computer that breaks down because its circuits are full of cracker crumbs.

. . .

DATA PROCESSOR'S LICENSE PLATE

ICALQL8

. . .

Did you hear about the new female computer?
You don't even have to ask it anything. It tells you anyhow.

. . .

Marketing execs who live in the better part of Palo Alto are whispered about like this: "Those yuppies never cry, they just Saab."

The mathematical wizards crowded before the great computer at the Technical Institute. "It's a mistake!" exclaimed one scientist. "No question of it. The computer made a mistake!"

The assembled geniuses passed the read-out tapes around, calculating, frowning, scrutinizing.

After a full hour of bafflement, the laboratory chief exclaimed, "Gentlemen, don't be discouraged. Do you realize it would take 6,300 mathematicians, working 14 hours a day, over 346 years to make a mistake like this?"

51

• • •

What do you get when you cross a computer with an alligator?

Either snappy answers or a computer with a byte.

• • •

Why was Isaac Newton knocked unconscious?

An Apple fell on his head.

• • •

Children are learning to use computers younger and younger. One company has a new model just for babies: Strained Apple.

• • •

SILICON SONG

She Was Only a Hacker's Daughter
but She Sure Knew How to Handle
Software

• • •

Do computers have good table manners?
Yes. They take very small bytes.

• • •

A start-up computer company was surprised one day by a Labor Department audit.

"Does everyone here make at least the minimum wage?"

"Oh, yes," said the entrepreneur, "except the half-wit."

"Oh?" snapped the inspector. "And what does the half-wit earn?"

"Let's see," said the owner. "I'd say it works out to about two bucks an hour, plus all the cold coffee he can drink, and a stale fruitcake at Christmas."

"Well," said the government man, "you just go bring this half-wit in here right now so I can talk to him."

"Don't have to," said the entrepreneur, "you're talking to him."

•   •   •

What do you get when you cross a computer with an onion?

Either a computer with a bad overflow problem, or answers that bring tears to your eyes.

•   •   •

Why was the computer cranky?
It was out of sorts.

•   •   •

"How long did you say your system's been down?"

How do computers choose their meals?
From menus, naturally!

• • •

What did one computer say to the other
before they parted?
"You're rotten to the core!"

• • •

There's a computer repair school in San
Francisco where the tuition is pretty steep.
It costs you about three thousand dollars to
learn to repair a set, so when you graduate,
you have to repair at least three computers
before you break even.

• • •

What do you call an aging programmer?
An old softie.

• • •

Why couldn't the computer find the information it was looking for?
It had a sloppy disk.

• • •

How many computers does it take to stop
an oncoming semi?
As many as possible.

Lee Felsenstein, the fabulous Golemics, Inc. guru, gets guffaws with this goofy glee-getter:

This was the first all-computerized flight to Mars. Five minutes after takeoff, the passengers heard this automated message:

"Welcome aboard, ladies and gentlemen. This flight is controlled by the latest, state-of-the-art, high-tech instrumentation. The temperature and pressure are monitored continuously. The course is navigated automatically. The meals are prepared and served by robot attendants. So just relax and enjoy the flight. Please be assured that absolutely nothing can go wrong . . . go wrong . . . go wrong . . ."

SIX PHASES OF A PROJECT

1. Enthusiasm
2. Disillusionment
3. Panic and hysteria
4. Search for the guilty
5. Punishment of the innocent
6. Praise and honor for the nonparticipants

• • •

There was a computer whose curse
Was to give every statement in verse.
  While some were just lewd,
  And others quite rude,
The logging-in message was worse.

• • •

What do you get when you cross a computer with a rabbit?
A computer that jumps to conclusions.

• • •

Why did the computer jump onto the chair?
It was scared by its mouse.

• • •

Why did the computer come down from the chair?
The cat ate its mouse.

Rojek, a young systems engineer on duty in the master control room of a gigantic electric power complex, was asked to demonstrate the operation to a group being shown through the plant. The visitor's host was the president of the company.

Rojek deftly threw switches, pressed buttons, and turned dials. Computer tapes whirled, lights flashed, electric arcs cracked across the room, and smoke poured out of the infernal apparatus. The engineer had wrecked the panel that controlled electric power to almost half of the U.S.A.

"Well, Rojek," barked the furious company prexy. "Now what are you going to do?"

"I'm going to buy a small farm in Iowa, sir!"

• • •

SILICON SLOGAN

If at first you don't succeed,
fail, fail again.

• • •

What do you get when you cross a computer with a mule?

A computer that gives you a cold boot when you plug it in.

• • •

Did you hear about the fully automated bank in Detroit?

A fellow sent it a card saying "This is a holdup," and the computer mailed the guy $200,000 in unmarked bills.

• • •

Byron went for a job interview as a computer terminal operator. However, the personnel director nearly fell off his chair when Byron told him he wanted a thousand dollars a week.

"You're nuts!" screamed the director. "You have absolutely no experience."

"That's right," Byron agreed, "and the job will be harder that way."

• • •

Steve Farson, fabulously funny Phoenix banker/comic, breaks up audiences with these selective sallies:

I saved money on my PC by buying it on a "Blue Light Special." Now I realize PC stands for piece of crap.

My new computer brochure says it's "user friendly." If you believe that, you'll also believe that Col. Qaddafi is the Welcome Wagon.

I bought a computer to help me manage my money and household finances. It's so reassuring to input my info once a month and have the computer tell me, "You are still broke."

• • •

Miss Kozinski, the secretary of a Michigan company, was given a word processor. The Polish girl couldn't use it after a week. The screen was covered with white-out.

• • •

What is a Polish word processor?
Two Hungarians with crayons and a Czech who knows how to spell.

• • •

What do you get when you cross an orchestra leader with a midget?
A semiconductor.

• • •

What does IBM stand for?
It's better manually.

• • •

"We're getting closer," said the guy from research and development. "This computer writes like Picasso and paints like Shakespeare."

• • •

What did the computer say to the adding machine?
"Anything you can do, I can do better!"

• • •

Fenwick made his decision. After months of agonizing over it, he finally bought a computer. Salkin, the salesman, assessed his needs and matched them to the lowest cost machine. Salkin then checked that Fenwick had everything he needed and knew how to operate the machine properly.

At home Fenwick loaded the program and

it booted perfectly. The software did everything promised.

A small problem developed with the printer interface. Fenwick phoned an 800 number and the expert diagnosed the problem, solved it, and even apologized for inconvenience.

In the two years since Fenwick bought his machine, he's saved enough time to build a scale model of Santa Clara out of bubble gum and toothpicks; cross-indexed every piece of junk mail he's received; listed all the household chores that need to be done before 1992 in order of their importance; and updated his Christmas card list.

Fenwick is so completely satisfied with his personal computer that not once has he regretted having spent too much too soon for an obsolete machine.

Modular Marrieds

The entire staff was gathered around a table as the meeting progressed. After an hour of dull and boring reports Elkins, a systems engineer, was reproached by the head of the company for daydreaming.

"Are you in love?" the boss asked the engineer sarcastically.

"Not a chance, sir," answered Elkins. "I'm married."

• • •

Healey went to a doctor and explained this his wife was constantly nagging him about his vanishing potency. The doctor performed surgery, providing Healey with a computerized penile implant. A month later, Healey returned.

"The implant is terrific," he said. "I've been doing it six, seven times a night."

"Wonderful," replied the physician. "What does your wife say about your love-making now?"

"I don't know!" said Healey. "I haven't been home yet."

• • •

Melissa was thrilled when she landed her first computer programming position. Her husband, Skip, although he knew nothing about the field, welcomed her at the door after the first day, inquiring, "What did you do at work today?"

He listened intently as she explained in great detail about her eight hours of COBOL, binary code, and JCL errors.

When she arrived home the next evening, Skip was once again at the front door. "So," he greeted her, "what did you have for lunch today?"

• • •

The newlyweds were undressing together for the first time in their hotel bedroom. The groom saw the bride looking at him appraisingly and, with an attempt at manly pride, puffed out his chest and beat on it saying, "A hundred and ninety pounds of solid mainframe."

"Yeah," said the bride, "with a little floppy disk!"

• • •

The computer nerd got married but did not consummate the marriage until a week after the wedding. The next morning he came into the office rubbing his hands together and happily said, "Wow, what a time I had with my wife last night!"

"What the hell did you wait so long for?" asked one of his buddies.

"How was I supposed to know she put out?"

• • •

Said a programmer bride to her groom,
"Let's stay in our nice little room.
    Movie prices are high."
    He exclaimed, "So am I!"
Then she did you know what to you
know whom.

• • •

The president of a Seattle semiconductor manufacturing firm had recently married a Las Vegas showgirl. His two friends, Vic and Eddie, were talking it over. "Well, he finally married her," said Vic. "He sure spent enough cash on gifts for her."

"Yes," said Eddie, "he married her for his money."

• • •

Young Dittner, a brilliant Stanford engineering grad, was waiting outside a hospital room for word about his wife. The doctor emerged from his examination of Mrs. Dittner to explain the sudden pain in her shoulder. The M.D. said gravely to the science genius, "I must tell you that your wife has acute angina."

"Yes, I know. But what's wrong with her shoulder?"

• • •

A computer fair producer married, and after the lavish wedding reception, he and the bride retired to their Ritz Carlton honeymoon suite in Laguna Niguel. The groom lowered the lights and found some romantic music on the radio. He excused himself and soon returned in pajamas and robe. He opened a bottle of champagne and poured them each a drink. Then he took his bride by the hand and tenderly led her toward the bedroom.

"Damn," she muttered, "every time I go out with a guy, it ends up the same way."

• • •

Malcolm and Arthur, both expectant fathers, nervously paced the floor in the waiting room of a San Jose maternity hospital.

"What tough luck," grumbled Malcolm. "This had to happen during my vacation."

"You think you've got troubles?" said Arthur. "I'm on my honeymoon."

• • •

SUBURBAN CORPORATE HUSBAND

A gardener with sex privileges.

• • •

The hacker honeymooners wanted to avoid the embarrassing attentions that most hotels bestow on newlyweds. They carefully removed the rice from their hair, took the Just Married sign off their Honda, and even scuffed their luggage to give it that traveled look. Then, without betraying a trace of their eagerness, they ambled casually up to the front desk at the Monterey Hyatt Hotel. The groom said in a loud, booming voice, "We'd like a double bed with a room."

Kalamazoo's John and Mary Hosley kid computer couples with this cajoler:

They were totally dedicated to their work. The husband was a hacker. The wife a programmer. Their jobs came first no matter what.

When Dr. Goodman delivered their bouncing baby boy, the infant was smiling from ear to ear. Goodman gave it a smack on its little behind, but instead of crying, the future electronics genius kept smiling.

Baffled, the obstetrician turned to his nurse, who pointed to the infant's right hand, which was clenched in a tight fist.

Dr. Goodman opened the little hand. Inside was The Pill.

As Boyd left for his Sunnyvale office, he called to Carol, his new bride, "Good-bye, Hollyhock!" She looked up that flower in a seed catalog to try to understand what he meant. It said: "Hollyhock—gay, colorful, and beautiful."

Carol phoned her mom to tell her the lovely compliment. The mother was suspicious and suggested she check it on their computer dictionary. Carol did. The screen flashed: "Rather common, does best under fences and around barns—poor in beds."

• • •

Harriet and Bob, newly married, moved to Seattle, where Bob went to work writing software programs. Harriet decided she should get a temporary job. Bouncing into the public library, she approached the attentive librarian sitting at the reference desk.

"Could you give me the name of a good book on positions?" she asked.

"What kind of positions did you have in mind?" asked the gray-haired librarian.

"Oh, you know," said the young girl, "the different kinds of positions a new bride might take."

• • •

"I liked it better when I was a football widow."

Newly married Damita was at her computer work station when she asked the machine, "What does the pain feel like when you have a baby?"

The computer flashed these instructions: "Take hold of lower lip and pinch as tight as possible."

Damita did it.

Then the machine instructed: "Now grasp firmly between thumb and forefinger and stretch lower-lip skin over skull and staple to back of neck."

• • •

Herman and Rita met at a microcomputer factory party. They eloped to Hollywood and the next day got on *Wheel of Fortune*. "How long have you been married?" asked the M.C.

"Sixteen hours and ten minutes," said the exhausted bride, "but it seems like about six months!"

"Why does it seem so long?"

"Well, I guess," replied Rita, "it's just that we've done so much in such a short time."

• • •

Agatha and Ryan were spending their honeymoon at the home of the bride's parents. Three days went by, and Agatha's young brother Jeffrey, a mechanical whiz kid, asked his mother why the newlyweds hadn't left their room, even to come down for meals. "It's none of your business," she replied.

A few more days passed, and the mother began to worry, too. Then she heard a commotion overhead, dashed upstairs to see what was going on, and discovered it was only Jeffrey rummaging through the bathroom.

"What are you looking for?" she inquired.

"Just my airplane glue," said the boy. "I've been keeping it in the Vaseline jar."

• • •

HAPPILY MARRIED SILICON COUPLE

A husband out with another man's wife.

• • •

Lee Bonnett, the Wyoming computer whiz, gets big boffs with this whopper:

Evans, a systems designer, had been preoccupied with a new project for over a year. He did nothing but talk about it twenty-four hours a day.

Finally his wife could stand it no longer. One night she said, "Can't we talk about something besides computers?"

"Sure," he said. "You pick the subject."

Without hesitation she said, "Let's talk about sex."

"Okay," said Evans. "You'll never guess who our programmer is sleeping with."

Bensen came home from his successful Phoenix computer company and found his wife in bed with another man.

"What is the meaning of this?" he thundered.

"Oh, didn't you know, darling," she laughed. "I've gone public, too."

Johnson, the marketing VP, just got back from vacation. "How do you feel?" asked an engineer.

"Okay," he replied, "except for jet nag."

"You mean jet lag, don't you?"

"I mean jet nag. My wife went with me."

• • •

Marlene was trying to get her husband to buy a computer but he didn't like the idea.

"What?" he roared. "Me buy a computer? Do you think computers grow on trees?"

"Don't be silly," she said. "Everyone knows they come from plants."

• • •

A bank offered personalized checks with the depositor's picture printed on them. Beekman took a picture of his wife in her bikini and had it printed on her new set of checks.

When he handed her the checkbook, she was furious. "That picture of me in a bikini is terrible!" she howled. "Do you think I'd cash one of these awful things?"

Beekman walked away, whistling softly to himself.

• • •

**"What does a woman like you see
in computers anyhow?"**

At the Xmas office party Campbell, the sales manager, headed for Della, the beautiful new engineer. He took her hand in his, kissed her fingers, and sighed his most effective sigh. Then he leaned over, gave her a peck on the neck, and whispered, "If you have no plans for the weekend, why don't you come to my country place? We'll have some fun."

"All right"—she smiled—"and I'll bring my boyfriend."

"Your boyfriend? What on earth for?"

"In case your wife wants to have some fun, too."

• • •

"Hey, Reg, heard you got a divorce. How come?"

"My wife called me an idiot."

"But that's not sufficient grounds for a divorce."

"Well, you see, I walked into my wife's office unexpectedly and found her in the arms of a computer service technician, so I said, 'What's the meaning of this?' and she said, 'Can't you see, you idiot?' "

• • •

SILICON VALLEY DIVORCÉE

Someone who spells relief
A-L-I-M-O-N-Y.

86

• • •

Corinne, a corporate exec, was so lusciously built that the computer technician just couldn't keep his eyes off her. When he'd finished servicing her laser writer, she hesitated and then said, "I'm going to make a—well—perhaps unusual request of you, but first you'll have to promise to keep it a strict secret."

"Okay," agreed the man.

"This is kind of embarrassing," said the woman, "but you see, while my boss is a fine, decent man, he unfortunately has—let me put it this way—a certain physical weakness, a certain disability. Now I'm a woman and you're a man—"

"Yes, yes," panted the technician.

"And since I've been wanting to do it for so long—well—would you please help me move the mainframe?"

• • •

Harlon, a bright young hacker, phoned Dr. Ruth to explain his troubles. "Every time I come home I find my wife making love to our neighbor on the living room couch."

"Well, what do you think you ought to do about it?" asked the popular sex adviser.

"That's my problem, Dr. Ruth. Do you think they could make trouble for me if I sold the couch?"

"Fantastic! I just broke into the DMV
computer and found out Doris Krebs is
three years older than I am!"

• • •

After several years of marriage, Peck, the youthful public relations exec, still couldn't keep away from other women. His wife was terribly jealous and Peck was fast running out of excuses to satisfy her. One afternoon he accompanied his pretty assistant to her apartment and made love to her far into the night.

Suddenly he looked at his watch and exclaimed, "My God, it's three o'clock in the morning." He quickly dialed his wife. When she answered the phone, Peck shouted, "Honey, don't pay the ransom. I've just escaped."

• • •

One cold Santa Clara Saturday morning, Calhoun spotted his neighbor Gallup, a design engineer, walking in his backyard. Gallup was wearing only a pajama top, nothing else.

"What's the idea?" asked Calhoun.

"I don't know," said the engineer. "The other day I walked over to the drugstore without a scarf and got a stiff neck. It's my wife's idea."

• • •

HACKER COFFEE BREAK

Scotty: How did you get that black eye?

Leo: My wife hung it on me because I was so absentminded. We went to a wedding and she asked me if I had kissed the bride.

Scotty: And she hit you because you said yes?

Leo: No, because I said, "Not lately."

• • •

Crandall was a first-rate hacker. He grew a shaggy beard. Wore old jeans to work. Consumed plenty of pizza and Cokes. His life was idyllic. Except for one thing. Crandall suspected his wife was cheating on him. He hired a detective to shadow her.

A week later the detective took Crandall home, where both peeked in through the door and saw Crandall's wife making love with a man.

Visibly shocked, Crandall invited the private eye into the kitchen, saying, "Let's have some coffee while I think."

"Thanks."

In the kitchen Crandall silently brewed two steaming cups of coffee. As they sat down to drink, the detective said, "Well, what about that guy in there?"

"The hell with him! Let him make his own coffee!"

Norman and Perry, two Silicon hackers, were wolfing pizza at Cicero's and talking about their married life. "Are you a man or a mouse?" asked Norman.

"I'm a mouse, and I'm the boss in my home," answered Perry.

"How can you be a mouse and be the boss in your home?"

"My wife is afraid of mice."

● ● ●

Worried about their lackluster sex life, Valerie finally persuaded her hacker husband to undergo hypnosis. After a few hypnosis treatments, his sexual interest began to improve, but during their lovemaking, he would dash out of the bedroom.

Overcome by curiosity, Valerie followed him to the bathroom. Tiptoeing to the doorway, she saw him standing before the mirror, staring at himself and muttering, "She's not my wife . . . she's not my wife . . ."

● ● ●

The Sinclairs wanted a child but not just an ordinary offspring. It had to be brilliant. One who could make a major contribution to the new world of technology.

The couple agreed to vacation near Stanford University in order to meet a Nobel computer scientist.

Sinclair, pretending to be only a friend, would encourage the genius to have a "one-shot" affair with his wife.

The project came off just as planned, and the husband waited with mixed emotions in the lobby of the motel, trying to console himself with dreams of the brainy child.

An hour later, he saw the computer wizard getting off the elevator and rushed up to him.

"How was it?" he asked.

"Oh, great," said the Nobel scientist casually, "but you know, she was so easy I just couldn't get over the feeling there might be something wrong—so I used a condom."

• • •

Did you know that seventy-five percent of all marriage rehearsals in the Silicon Valley are not held in churches?

• • •

Melton, a venture capitalist, wasn't feeling well and went to Dr. Daniels for a checkup.

After the examination the physician said, "Either you stop smoking, drinking, and having sex, or you'll be dead in twelve months."

Three weeks later Melton went back and said, "Look, I'm so miserable I might just as well be dead. *Please,* can I smoke just a little?"

"Very well, just five filter tips a day," said the medic.

In three weeks Melton was back again. "Look, I really miss my martinis—please . . .?"

"All right, just two drinks a day."

Time went by, and the patient approached the doctor for the third time. "Listen, I gotta have some sex."

"Yes, yes, but only with your wife—no excitement!"

• • •

Royce was considered the sharpest programmer in the company. Everybody loved his wit and charm, especially the young secretaries. Royce had been cheating on his wife for years. One night he arrived home in the wee hours, crept into the bedroom, and began undressing. His wife, who'd been watching him out of the corner of her eye, cried, "Royce! Where's your underwear?"

"My God!" he exclaimed. "I've been robbed!"

Adam Osborne, the incomparable Osborne computer founder, furnished this gleeful funny:

Jack's wife lay on her deathbed. After the priest had given her the last rites, her husband asked to be alone with her.

"Darling, I have a confession to make," she whispered. "I'm the one who took money from your safe. I spent it on a fling with your best friend. I'm the one who sold your company computer secrets to your competitor."

"Don't worry about such things now," said Jack.

"There's more. I'm the one who blackmailed your mistress to leave town. I hope you forgive me for everything."

"There's nothing to forgive," answered Jack. "We're even. I'm the one who poisoned you."

Dougherty had been working late on a program with some of the engineers at the company. They finally quit and stopped for some drinks.

Dougherty arrived home stoned to the gills. Since he couldn't find the key to the front door, he began climbing through the window. He was almost inside when a policeman stopped him.

"Sure this is my house!" Dougherty blubbered, pulling the cop in after him. "This is my hall, that's my carpet, this is my bedroom, that's my bed, that's my wife, and you see that guy in bed with her? That's me!"

• • •

Late one night a Galveston salesman answered the phone: "How do I know? Why don't you call the weather bureau?"

"Who was that?" inquired his beautiful young wife.

"Don't know. Some damned fool wanted to know if the coast was clear."

• • •

The computer salesman was demonstrating his highest-priced system to a couple. "What do you think?" he asked.

"I could certainly do a lot of things with it," replied the wife. "But then again, I said the same thing the first time I looked at my husband.''

• • •

Why did the married computers get a divorce?

They kept getting Type Mismatch messages on their screens.

• • •

When hacker Chapman came home at four in the morning, he saw his wife in the arms of another man. She cried to her husband, ''Where have you been till four in the morning?''

And he shouted, ''Who is that man?''

She said, ''Don't change the subject!''

• • •

Gavin told his coworker Tully that his wife was suspicious of his carrying on. ''When I go home tonight, I know she'll start giving me hell!''

That night, she said, ''I know you're fooling around with other women. Is it my friend Emily or that widow Amy or my hairdresser Nicole?''

The next day Tully said, ''Did she bawl you out last night?''

''Yeah,'' said Gavin, ''but boy, did she give me three swell leads.''

"My Michael is bilingual. He also
speaks Computerese."

• • •

Stella, a software marketing VP who traveled a lot, became suspicious of her husband, Roy, and hired a detective agency to keep tabs on him. When she returned from her next trip, Stella went to the agency's headquarters. They showed her photos and videotapes and tape recordings of Roy with one of her friends.

She saw her husband having glamorous nights on the town, meeting in motels, swimming in the nude, hugging and kissing and laughing.

"It's hard to believe," sighed the executive.

"About your friend's involvement?" asked the detective.

"No, I could believe anything of her," mumbled Stella, "but I can't believe my husband could be that much fun!"

User-Friendly Funnies

Barton, a New York bachelor living on West 79th Street, took his computer to a place on York Avenue that advertised twenty-four-hour service.

"When should I pick it up?" he asked.

"Next Thursday," said the man.

"A week from today?" snapped Barton. "I thought you had twenty-four-hour service."

"We do," said the repairman. "We work eight hours Monday, eight hours Tuesday, and eight hours Wednesday."

• • •

Why won't computers ever replace newspapers?
Have you ever tried to swat a fly with a
computer?

• • •

What do you call a monastic who works
on integrated circuits?
A chipmonk.

• • •

What do you call a robot ape?
A chipanzee.

• • •

Dan Marrone sent in this doozie:

How do you praise an accurate computer?
"Data boy!"

• • •

What do you get when you cross a computer with a blender?
A mixed solution.

• • •

What kind of PC does a woman carry in
her purse?
A Compacqt.

"How's that for user friendly!"

• • •

Barbara Leeds, the magnificent Mountain View mirthmaker, lent this loony limerick:

Computerdom's whiz kid, named
    Douglas
Insisted his programs were bugless—
    Which got a good laugh
    From the rest of the staff,
And now the department is Doug-less.

• • •

What did the digital clock say to its mother?
"Look, Ma! *No hands!*"

• • •

What do you get when you cross an IBM and a comedian?
Buddy Hacker.

• • •

What do computers do for fun?
They stand around and give each other wrong answers.

• • •

Danny had two loves: chemistry and his computer. One day while driving nails into a board, Danny's father asked, "What are you doing with those nails?"

"They're not nails, Dad. My computer came up with this chemical formula. I put some on these worms and they get hard as nails."

Father's eyes brightened. "Make me some of that stuff and I'll buy you that new laser printer you wanted."

Danny gave him a bottle of the concoction, and sure enough, two days later he had a new laser printer plus a new Macintosh SE.

"Thanks for the printer, Dad, but what's the Mac for?"

"That's for you, too, Son. It's a present from your mother."

Peter Nixon, the Avid Productions mastermind, says, "If computers get too powerful, we can organize them into committees. That would set them back some."

· · ·

WORD PROCESSOR

A typewriter without bread crumbs.

· · ·

What do you get when you cross a computer with a midget?
A short circuit.

· · ·

Can computers run away from home?
Not unless someone plugs them in.

· · ·

NANOSECOND NURSERY RHYME

Star light, star bright
First star I see tonight.
I wish I may, I wish I might
. . . Oh, no, it's a satellite!

· · ·

A recent *New Yorker* cartoon shows a detective telling a potential client, "I'm an old-fashioned private eye, Miss Jones. If this little mystery of yours has anything to do with computers, forget it."

• • •

Then there's the Sidney Harris cartoon showing a businessman with a new computer on his desk. He is telling his secretary, "It does data processing, word processing, and list processing. Get me some dates, some words, and some lists."

• • •

How many software engineers does it take to screw in a light bulb?
None. That's a hardware problem.

• • •

What back problem do computers have?
Slipped disks.

• • •

What's a computer's most common dental problem?
Malocclusion, or overbyte.

• • •

"It's true we advertised for a retriever, but . . ."

The Texas Ranger didn't know quite how to break the awful news to the woman. When she answered the doorbell, he said, "Miz Daniels, I'm Officer Nolan."

"Howdy," she said.

"You know that new Stetson you bought your husband?"

"Yes . . . ?" said the woman.

"Well, it's been ruined."

"Ruined! How?"

The officer replied, "A mainframe fell on it."

• • •

Where did the Bionic Man go to college?
Solid State.

• • •

COMPUTER TV SHOW

Murder, She Word-Processed

• • •

Bill Mollard, the magnetic Computerland mastermind came up with this humdinger:

Trying to sell his newest computer to Barrett, a young businessman, the salesman invited his skeptical client to ask it a question. The executive sat down and typed out his query: "Where is my father?"

The machine rapidly printed the reply: "Your father is fishing in Michigan."

"This contraption doesn't know what it's talking about," bellowed Barrett. "My father's been dead for twenty years."

Certain that his creation was infallible, the salesman suggested, "Why don't you ask the same question in a different form?"

Barrett typed: "Where is my mother's husband?"

The computer answered: "Your mother's husband has been dead for twenty years. Your father has just landed a three-pound trout."

What did the mother computer say to her sick baby?

"Never mind, dear. We'll soon have those nasty bugs out of your system."

* * *

What's a sure sign of old age in a computer?

Loss of memory.

* * *

How does a computer die?

It comes down with a terminal illness.

* * *

Old Mrs. Vanderhoff walked into the credit department at American Express and demanded, "I don't care to bandy words with underlings about my overdue account. Take me to your computer."

* * *

The giant computer took up an entire wall, dwarfing Rick and Stacy standing next to it. After much beeping and flashing, it handed them a sliver of paper. "Do you realize," said Rick, "it would take four hundred ordinary mathematicians over two hundred and fifty years to make a mistake this big?"

"Computer still down?"

113

• • •

Gary Jackson came up with a new senior citizen software program:

It reminds you what you had for breakfast, tells you what year it is, tells you how many grandchildren you have, lists each one's name and current address, and shows you whether or not you have a pulse.

• • •

What's a computer's favorite song?
"Thanks for the Memory."

• • •

COMPUTER MOVIE

Love at First Byte

• • •

Why did they fire the computer that worked for the Sanitary Department?
Garbage in, garbage out.

• • •

What did the computer say about its illness when it got better?
"Boy, that really knocked me for a loop."

Did you hear about the agnostic hacker?

He hocked everything he owned to build his home computer into the world's most powerful machine. Then he plugged it into every data bank, let it invade every library, and had it read every book. Finally he typed in the question:

"Computer, is there a god?"

The computer flashed, the screen flickered, and finally the machine responded: "There is now!"

• • •

In Chicago for a computer convention Bob and Vera were seated at the Palmer House bar. A drunk sitting near them suddenly let out a big fart. Bob snapped, "How dare you fart before my wife!"

"I'm sorry," said the drunk, "I didn't know it was her turn."

• • •

Did you hear about the newest computer that's almost human?

When it makes a mistake, it can put the blame on another computer.

• • •

"Homeroom monitor certainly has changed
since I was a student."

And another Barbara Leeds beaut:

Have you heard of that programmer, Ron,
Whose memory circuits are gone?
   His brain turned to soup
   From an infinite loop,
And no one can turn him back on.

· · ·

God was speaking to Moses.

"I'm going to give you the Ten Commandments on two tablets," said the Almighty.

"Thank you," said Moses.

"I would have given them to you on software, but I didn't know whether you had an Apple or an IBM!"

· · ·

What did the big computer say to the little computer?

"Power down, kid. You don't have enough chips for this game!"

· · ·

How do computers cook?
In microwave ovens.

· · ·

The preacher decided to enumerate the Ten Commandments to his flock. When he got to the fourth, "Thou shalt not steal," he noticed Peck, a hacker in the first row, acting nervously. When the preacher got to the seventh, "Thou shalt not commit adultery," he saw Peck suddenly brighten up and smile.

After the services the preacher approached Peck and asked him the reason for his strange conduct. The happy hacker replied, "When you told the fourth commandment, 'Thou shalt not steal,' I remembered that my laptop computer was missing. But when you said, 'Thou shalt not commit adultery,' I remembered where I left it."

119

BUMPER STICKER

Computer Operators Do It
With Hard Drives

• • •

Will computers ever drive cars?
They will if they can pass the driver's license test.

• • •

A computer had just been installed in a company and the boss was a nervous wreck worrying about it. One afternoon he approached a secretary sitting in front of a monitor doing her nails.

"Why isn't that computer working?" he snapped.

The woman replied, "The little person inside is taking a coffee break."

• • •

How do you know when your computer is angry?
It'll have a chip on its shoulder.

• • •

Where do computers like to stroll when they have a class reunion?
Down memory lane.

• • •

Business was so good at his clothing store Bernstein decided to move to larger and nicer quarters. He had an open house and received flowers from all his friends. The card on one bunch of flowers read "Rest in Peace."

Bernstein phoned the florist and asked, "What's going on?"

"Don't ask!" said the florist. "Our computer screwed up. Somewhere there's a funeral with flowers and a card that reads 'Good Luck in Your New Location.'"

• • •

ODE TO THE COMPUTER

We shall have to design
Computers galore
Since each problem they solve
Creates ten million more.

• • •

The Dugans were having dinner.

"Remember the salesman who said I could learn to use the computer in two weeks?" asked the husband.

"Yes, dear," said the wife.

"He got the bill wrong, too."

• • •

Mark and Henry, two component assemblers, were telling each other the dreams they'd had the night before. Mark said he dreamed he was in Atlantic City having a wonderful time playing blackjack.

Henry said, "I dreamed I was alone in a room with Vanna White. And as if that wasn't enough, who should walk in but Racquel Welch."

"A fine buddy you are," said Mark. "Why didn't you phone me?"

"I did," said Henry. "I phoned you in my dream. But your wife said you were in Atlantic City."

• • •

How many computer salesmen does it take to screw in a light bulb?

"I'll get back to you."

• • •

Walsh and Reese, two computer salesmen, were sipping morning coffee.

"What's the latest dope on PCs?" asked Walsh.

"My son," replied Reese.

• • •

"How many times do I have to tell you,
garbage in, garbage out!"

When is a computer most ungrateful?
When it bytes the hand that feeds it.

• • •

Electronics whiz Gary Rubio loves this rib-buster:

Four engineers were discussing the high intelligence of their dogs. The IBM engineer said his dog "T Square" could do math calculations. He told her to go to the blackboard and draw a square, a circle, and a triangle. The dog did it.

The Epson engineer told his dog "Slide Rule" to fetch a dozen cookies, bring them back, and divide them into four piles of three each. The canine followed instructions to the letter.

The Atari engineer said his dog "Pokey" was smarter. He told him to get a quart of milk and pour seven ounces into a ten-ounce glass. The animal did as his master bid.

The Apple engineer called to his dog "Coffee Break" and said, "Show these guys what you can do."

Coffee Break went over and ate the cookies, drank the milk, screwed the other three dogs, claimed he injured his back, filed for workmen's compensation, and went home on sick leave.

Corporate Cackles

The CEO of a semiconductor company called all his employees together on Monday morning. "Gang, I want you to know I'm exactly like you," he began. "I am not always right—but I'm never wrong."

Then he added, "If you have something to complain about, I want you to speak right out—even if it costs you your job."

• • •

Blaney and Wilkins, vice presidents of a PC company, were having lunch. "You know our new programmer, Agnes?" asked Blaney. "Did you ever have an affair with her?"

"No," said Wilkins.

"Did you ever take her out for lunch?"

"No."

"Did you ever give her a present or call her up after office hours?"

"Absolutely not!" stated Wilkins.

"Good," sighed Blaney. "Then you'll have to be the one to fire her."

• • •

CONSULTANT

Someone who is called in at the last moment to share the blame.

• • •

Dutton wandered about the store examining each Hewlett-Packard, Zenith, and Leading Edge machine. Finally the corporate VP stopped at a Macintosh SE.

"Now that little baby," said the sales clerk, "will do half your job for you."

"Great!" said the exec. "I'll take two."

127

" UHH - OOH ! "

Did you hear about the CEO whose bonus was up to six figures?

The board of trustees.

• • •

Jordan, a Dallas computer company exec, arrived at his house before lunch. "What're you doing home so early, dear?"

"I had a fight with the boss," admitted Jordan. "He wouldn't take back what he said."

"Oh, my!" sighed the woman. "What did he say?"

"You're fired!"

• • •

A fellow had trouble with his head. A team of brain surgeons agreed to remove his brain, examine it, then put it back later. They performed the operation, but when they came to put his brain back, he wasn't there. The man had disappeared. A month later he returned to the happy doctors.

"Where have you been since we removed your brain?"

"I became a consultant at Hewlett-Packard."

• • •

Dave Arnold, the Sonoma State University computer genius, gets shrieks with this side-splitter:

Feldman, the sales manager, stood before an assembled group in a corporate conference room. They were there to observe a demonstration of his company's state-of-the-art computer.

The rep's screen blurred and rolled. His attempt at a telecommunication link failed. Feldman phoned his company for help, but his liaison was gone for the day. That's when he faced the group and said, "This concludes my demonstration of our competitor's product. Next week I'll come back and show you ours."

An efficiency expert took charge of a big semiconductor company. After he had been there awhile, the employees decided to hold a picnic in the efficiency expert's honor and award prizes. They started to sell tickets for the event.

One systems engineer refused to buy a ticket, crying, "I'd rather knock his teeth down his throat."

"Swell. That's the first prize."

· · ·

Barlow, a young electronics executive, was sipping a martini in a bar when he noticed an attractive woman seated beside him. His interest must have been obvious because the bartender suddenly loomed over him and said, "Don't get any ideas about that girl, Mac. That's my wife."

Barlow said, "Who's getting ideas? I just came in for a piece of beer."

· · ·

Phillip, a marketing exec, and his wife, Jeanne, were trapped in the elevator of a Sunnyvale condo building. After ten minutes they were getting desperate.

"Too bad you can't phone one of the programmers at the office," said Jeanne. "They could tell us what to do!"

"Listen," said Phillip, "I've got an idea.

What about crawling out the top of the elevator, sliding down the cable, and forcing open the door on the floor below. How does that sound?''

"It sounds dangerous," said the wife.

"Then don't do it."

• • •

The president of a new PC company gave a speech at a banquet honoring the governor. He said, "We turn out one of our new computers complete in every detail in two minutes."

An article appeared in the newspapers, and the next day a fellow called up the PC prexy and asked, "Is it true that you said you turn out a computer, complete in every detail, in two minutes?"

"Yes."

"Damn you. I've got that computer."

• • •

A computer salesman was boasting to another salesman, "I just got an order for a hundred thousand dollars from Macy's."

The other said, "I don't believe it."

"You don't believe it? Here, I'll show you the cancellation."

• • •

"A trillionth of a second here, a trillionth of a second there. These damned delays will kill you."

• • •

The country's most proficient microprocessor producer left the banquet hall with a look of self-satisfaction. One of his colleagues stopped him and said, "Congratulations, Clayborn!"

"Thank you, thanks very much."

"Were you surprised when you got the nomination as president of the new computer association?"

"I'll say. My acceptance speech nearly fell right out of my hand."

• • •

The president of a firm that produced microprocessors walked into a shoe store one afternoon and said, "Give me a pair of shoes two sizes too small."

"Two sizes too small?" asked the sales clerk. "What's the idea?"

"I got trouble. Nothing but trouble. The Koreans have come up with a computer that's IBM compatible and sells for two hundred and fifty dollars, my partner is leaving me to join another company, and I've been threatened with two lawsuits. So, the only pleasure I have left is to go home at night and take off my tight shoes."

• • • •

Baldwin, the sales exec, had checked out of his hotel room and was leaving for the airport in a cab. Suddenly he realized that he had left his computer in his room. Fortunately he had neglected to turn in his key, so he rushed back up to the room.

But as Baldwin turned the key, he heard voices. The room had already been rented. He heard sighs and moans and then a man spoke.

"Whose little toes are they?"

"Yours," said a female.

"And whose little knees are they?" asked the man.

"Yours," said the girl.

"And whose little thighs are they?" asked the man.

"Yours, all yours," moaned the girl.

Baldwin said, "When you come to a Compaq Portable III, it's mine."

"And the incredible thing about it is
this neat little slot where I can keep my yo-yo."

They were all gathered together in the conference room. Suddenly a hush fell over the group.

"Team, all that time and effort and money has finally paid off!" said the chief engineer. "I wonder if there's an actual market for this?"

. . .

Two microchip executives were considering their sluggish business.

"You know the difference between computers and the *Titanic*?" said one.

"No," said the other.

"The *Titanic* had entertainment."

. . .

Haynes, the software executive, said to his departing secretary, "In a way I'll be sorry to lose you. You've been like a daughter to me—insolent, surly, unappreciative."

. . .

Conversational gem from Houston:

"Well, the deal is set. All we're waiting for now is a yes-or-no answer."

. . .

Drake, a systems engineer, left Cupertino and went to Paris for the first time. When he returned home after his exciting trip, another engineer asked for his impression of Paris.

"Such buildings and streets we haven't got in Cupertino. I was walking down the Champs-Élysées boulevard and this really pretty French girl winked at me. That never happened to me in Cupertino. Then she took me to an outdoor café and bought a drink for me. Believe me, that never happened in Cupertino. Then she took me up to her apartment and we had some more drinks. That, I can tell you, never happened to me in Cupertino. In a few minutes she started to take off her clothes. And then it was exactly like in Cupertino."

• • •

Marlin, the marketing exec, was bedding down Arlene, a young software programmer, at a motel. As they embraced, he said, "You realize this isn't just a physical thing. This is a union of minds."

"It's our minds?" she said.

"Yes, yes," said Marlin. "It's an intellectual attraction that's uniting us."

"It's not just the ordinary thing?" said Arlene.

"No, no," said the exec. "And you know something?—it's every bit as good."

140

"The good news is your computer is not broken.
The bad news is, I think it's in heat."

Concerned about the dangers of crime in the streets, Harris, a corporate VP, enrolled in a karate school. Next day he told an associate about his first lesson.

"It was actually a lot of fun," said the executive. "As soon as you get there, you put on pajamas and start yelling hysterically."

"Reminds me of my honeymoon," said his friend.

• • •

The boss's wife tiptoed into the office behind him and kissed him behind the ear.

"Guess who!" she said.

"I've told you we don't have time for that. Now get those letters out!"

• • •

"Is being on an upper management level more secure jobwise?"

"You kidding? There's so much executive shuffling at the big computer companies they're lettering names on executive doors in chalk."

• • •

Have you noticed that there have been fewer office parties this year? Who wants to kiss a computer?

• • •

An efficiency expert, making a survey of a company office in Santa Clara, noted that there were more desks and phones than personnel. He asked a secretary, "What's the usual complement of this office?"

"Usually it's, 'Where do we go, baby, your place or mine?' "

* * *

A large Massachusetts semiconducter corporation was holding its annual meeting of department heads. The chairman of the board turned to Pearson, the personnel manager, and asked, "How many people do we now employ, broken down by sex?"

"Sir," said Pearson, "I'm glad to say, not too many. Liquor is more of a problem with us!"

* * *

Elton had long ceased to be useful and the boss finally fired him. "Who are you going to get to fill my vacancy?"

The boss shrugged. "You're not leaving a vacancy."

* * *

Carlson, a microcomputer company VP suffering from ringing in his ears, went to a doctor who recommended that his tonsils be removed. The operation didn't help. Another doctor suggested his teeth be extracted. Still the ringing continued.

Finally, a third specialist told him bluntly, "I'm sorry, but you're suffering from a rare disease. At best you have six months to live."

Since Carlson had no relatives, he decided to spend all his money. He booked passage for a trip around the world and had twenty suits made by the best tailor. Carlson even decided to have his shirts made to order.

"All right," said the shirtmaker, "let's get your measurements. Thirty-four sleeve, sixteen collar—"

"No, that's fifteen," said the exec.

"Collar sixteen," repeated the shirtmaker.

The VP insisted, "I've always worn a fifteen collar and that's what I want."

"All right," said the shirtmaker, "but you'll get a ringing in your ears."

Peripheral Persiflage

How do you make a computer laugh?
Tell it a programmer joke.

* * *

An ambitious young woman, filling out a job application at a PC company, pondered the last question on the form: "What are your aims and ambitions?"

Finally she wrote: "I want to go as far as my education and sex will allow."

* * *

What did the computer say to the bank teller?

"You can count on me!"

.   .   .

What should you do with a computer that's a year old?

Wish it a happy birthday.

.   .   .

What does a computer wipe his feet on?

His format.

.   .   .

In a Radio Shack store an elderly man took a playing stance and expectantly gripped the sides of a machine.

"How do you play this thing?" he yelled at the clerk.

"You don't," said the clerk. "That's a battery tester."

.   .   .

"I think maybe machines are taking over the world."

"Why do you say that?"

"This morning I found a message on our computer screen. It said: 'To err is human.'"

.   .   .

"Repeat after me. DOS rhymes with sauce
and ROM rhymes with prom."

Where are computer soldiers stationed?
In a Fortran.

• • •

Blelock and Moore, two microcomputer
manufacturing moguls, were munching lunch
at the Lion and Compass.

"I tell you," said Blelock, "every day
the modern businessman is faced with new
and unique problems."

"Right on!" agreed Moore.

"We just had to let our senior programmer go. Tell me, how do you get a computer in trouble?"

• • •

An Apple a day may keep the doctor
away, but not the IRS.

• • •

Where do computers go dancing?
To a disk-o-tech.

• • •

Did you hear about the new job a computer got?

It posed for the centerfold in *Popular
Mechanics*.

• • •

Humor collector Casey Roche contributed this cutie:

All measures of time had some correspondence to events found in nature, ranging from the time it takes the earth to circle the sun, to some fraction of a wave length of part of the spectrum. But the "fempto second," one trillionth of one second, had still stumped scientists.

Finally, after months of dedicated research, they made the announcement:

"A 'fempto second' is the amount of time that elapses in New York between the light's turning green and the guy behind you honking."

"You guys in microprocessor manufacturing must be making a fortune."

"Don't be nuts! The only people making money these days are the ones who sell computer paper."

• • •

The average hacker is thirty-six around the chest, forty around the waist, ninety-eight around the golf course, and a nuisance around the house.

• • •

Many pharmaceutical firms supply drugstores with order forms listing products and their costs. When one company neglected to do this despite repeated requests, an employee attached this note to an order: "Your computer and I have been having communication problems. If you no longer supply order forms, please let us know . . . that is, if you still employ real people."

With the next delivery there was this note: "Enclosed please find six order forms. Please forgive the delay. Yes, we still employ people. Therein lies the problem." Signed, "IBM 402."

• • •

"Give me all your chips!"

Henderson, who was running for mayor, visited an office where they had several computers set up to monitor election returns. A woman came up with the estimated results and said, "The computer says you will win, but that personally it would not vote for you."

* * *

CHICAGO TV NEWSCASTER

"In today's election, with only one hundred and thirty-four percent of the vote in, the computers have been able to accurately predict a winner."

* * *

A chip manufacturer employee was called on the carpet for talking back to his department head.

"Is it true that you called him a liar?"

"Yes, I did."

"Did you call him stupid?"

"Yes."

"And did you call him an opinionated, bullheaded egomaniac?"

"No, but would you write that down so I can remember it?"

* * *

Pierce walked into the house in a state of total exhaustion. "Darling," exclaimed his wife, "you look terrible. What's the matter?"

"It was a terrible day at the office, dear," he replied. "The computer stopped and we all had to think."

• • •

The famous computer wizard came home at eight one morning and told his wife he had been up most of the night at a brainstorming session. Afterward, he had driven his secretary home. He explained further that she had asked him in for a cup of coffee and then kindly offered to put him on her sofa for the remainder of the night because it was so late.

His wife looked at him angrily. "Don't lie to me," she said. "I know you were fooling around with your Leading Edge again!"

• • •

The computer store salesman admitted to being flustered for just a minute. It seems a dewy-eyed damsel asked for a software program titled, "How to Make Friends and Influential People."

• • •

The average hacker has probably thought twice about running away from home—once as a child and once as a husband.

* * *

Dr. Norby, the psychiatrist, had been treating Pendleton for several years for a severe case of kleptomania. It seems the man would steal anything he could lay his hands on. Now the shrink pronounced him cured.

"I can hardly believe it!" said the grateful man.

"Yes," said the analyst, "I believe we now have your kleptomania under control. You can go out into the world just like anybody else."

"It's wonderful!" sniffed Pendleton. "I don't know how to repay you."

"My fee is all the payment I expect," said the doctor. "However, if you should happen to have a relapse, you might pick up a Compaq Portable III for me."

* * *

COMPUTER

A machine that performs complex calculations in one ten-thousandth of a second—and mails out statements ten days late.

* * *

Fenton went into a video game store. A sign over a computer said "Conversation: 50¢." He put in half a buck and the screen lit up with the question: "What's your IQ?"

Fenton typed in "110." The computer whirred and then carried on a conversation with him for three minutes before turning off. Fenton put in another half dollar.

The computer again asked: "What's your IQ?"

This time Fenton replied "180."

The computer then started talking to him about quantum physics, fourth-dimensional theories, and deep existentialist issues. Fenton could barely respond sensibly until finally the computer turned off.

Fenton put in another fifty cents.

Again the computer requested his IQ level. This time Fenton replied. "621."

The computer answered quickly: "Time for your nap, Ronnie."

• • •

Did you hear about the new Las Vegas computer doll?

You wind it up and it spits out chips!

• • •

Bolton was looked upon as the best programmer in the company. Sometimes he worked until three in the morning on a project. Recognizing his technological skill, everyone overlooked his quirky and idiosyncratic behavior.

One day Bolton went to the doctor for a checkup. "Stick out your tongue and say 'ah,' " directed the doctor.

Bolton did as he was told.

"Your tongue looks all right, but why the postage stamp?" asked the medico.

"Oh," cried the computer freak, "so that's where I left it!"

• • •

How many hackers does it take to change a light bulb?

Five.

One to steal a shipment of arc lamps going to the Louisiana Superdome.

One to install a six-ton air handler and cooling system.

One to reroute the voltage lines from his neighborhood to Mexico, causing a brownout throughout Canada.

One to rewire the house with sixteen-inch coaxial cable.

One to unscrew the old bulb to substitute the greater light source.

• • •

APPLE
COMPUTER
INC.

IN CASE
OF
EMERGENCY

BREAK
GLASS

160

PROGRAMMER'S PRAYER

Dear Lord, please protect us from "intellectual arrogance" . . . which for your information may be defined as follows . . .

• • •

Mrs. Whiting was shopping at the supermarket when her neighbor, Mrs. Swett, stopped her. "Say," Mrs. Swett asked, "who was that young lady I saw with you and your husband yesterday?"

"That was no young lady," replied Mrs. Whiting. "That was our son, Robert, the programmer. I always wanted a child with long blond curls—but I had hoped it would be a girl."

• • •

A Kansas City mother shouted to her young son, "Why is your floppy disk on the davenport."

The boy replied, "What's a davenport?"

• • •

COMPUTER

A thinking machine that's almost human, except that it hasn't learned yet to swear, drink, or gamble.

• • •

Mosby sat at the desk of the large computer company's personnel director. "You want a job in this company?" he asked. "What can you do?"

"Nothing."

"I'm sorry. All those high-salaried positions were taken long ago."

• • •

Bristow, Morgan, and Archer, three programmers, were sitting in a railroad station waiting for a train. They were so absorbed in discussing computer technology that they failed to notice the arrival of the train.

Suddenly, Bristow spotted the train as it started to pull out, and they all rushed for it. Morgan and Archer caught the train. Bristow missed it.

A bystander said to Bristow, "Don't feel too bad. At least two of you made it."

"Yes, I know," said the electronics whiz, "but those two came down to see me off."

• • •

Farmer Bradshaw went to the doctor to get his elbow looked at. The nurse gave him a bottle for a urine sample. "But I only got a crick in my elbow," said Bradshaw.

"We've got a new computer," said the

nurse. "With a urine sample it can detect a person's problems and prescribe proper treatment."

She told him to take the bottle home, fill it, and bring it back for the computerized analysis.

The farmer put a little sample in the jar, he had his wife put some in, then his daughter, then his son put some in, and he even got a sample of the dog's urine. Then he took the bottle back to the doctor's office.

Ten minutes later the nurse handed him the computer printout. It read: "Your wife is pregnant. Your son has VD. Your dog has worms. Your daughter is screwing everybody in town. And if you don't stop playing with yourself, you're going to develop a bad crick in the elbow."

• • •

Rolf and Paul, two marketing execs, were having breakfast at the Peppermill.

"I just got a Zenith Z One Five Nine computer for my wife," announced Rolf.

"Gosh," said Paul, "I wish I could make a deal like that!"

• • •

What do you call a transsexual nun?
A transsister.

• • •

163

MENU MOTTO

The program that never failed on your last computer will never run on your current computer.

● ● ●

What do you get when you cross a computer with an elephant?
A five-ton know-it-all.

● ● ●

Janet had just graduated from UC Berkeley. She was looking forward to her first day on the job as a market researcher for a high-tech firm. However, she quit after doing her first interview.
When she asked the subject whether he thought ignorance and apathy were the greatest problems facing the world today, he answered, "I don't know and I don't care."

● ● ●

What is a computer freak's seven-course dinner?
Six cans of Pepsi Cola and a jelly doughnut.

● ● ●

"Two double-density floppy disks,
one large order of Silicon chips,
and your sister's phone number, please!"

Talbot turned to his scatterbrained secretary and said, "Miss Grundy, you've already been here two months. Don't you think it's time you learned to use a computer?"

"If you insist," replied the young woman, "but I still think it's easier to play tic-tac-toe on paper!"

• • •

JUNK FOOD JUNKIE

A hacker who thinks natural food is carrot cake without the icing.

• • •

Gerald and Cynthia were both computer science majors. After graduation they began work at the same company as programmers. It was only natural that they marry.

Two weeks after their honeymoon a friend asked Gerald, "Haven't you lost a lot of weight?"

"Yeah, neither one of us can cook."

"What about TV dinners?"

"Well," said Gerald, "we can't figure out how to keep from burning them in the toaster."

"Why don't you use the microwave?"

"Then where would we dry the laundry?"

What is a hacker's four-star restaurant?
A room full of vending machines.

• • •

While Milgrom waited at the airport for his plane to depart, he noticed a computer scale that gave your weight and your fortune for a quarter. He dropped a coin in the slot and the computer screen displayed: "You weigh 195 pounds, you're married, and you're on your way to San Diego."

Milgrom stood there dumbfounded.

Another man put in a quarter and the computer read: "You weigh 184 pounds, you're divorced, and you're on your way to Chicago."

Milgrom asked the man, "Are you divorced and on your way to Chicago?"

"Yes," replied the man. Milgrom shook his head in amazement.

Just then another man tried the computer. It responded with: "You weigh 165 pounds, you're single, and you're on your way to Miami."

Milgrom said, "Excuse me, are you single and on your way to Miami?"

"Yeah," answered the man.

Milgrom rushed into the men's room, changed his clothes, put on dark glasses, pulled down his hat, turned up his collar, sneaked up on the machine, and dropped in the coin. The computer read: ''You still weigh 195 pounds, you're still married, on your way to San Diego. And idiot! You just missed your plane!''

LARRY WILDE

Here's how to start your own Larry Wilde humor library!!!

DON'T MISS
THESE CURRENT
Bantam Bestsellers

Special Offer
Buy a Bantam Book
for only 50¢.

Now you can have Bantam's catalog filled with hundreds of titles plus take advantage of our unique and exciting bonus book offer. A special offer which gives you the opportunity to purchase a Bantam book for only 50¢. Here's how!

By ordering any five books at the regular price per order, you can also choose any other single book listed (up to a $5.95 value) for just 50¢. Some restrictions do apply, but for further details why not send for Bantam's catalog of titles today!

Just send us your name and address and we will send you a catalog!